Marijuana: Facts, Figures, & Opinions

marijuana today

marijuana today

Marijuana: Facts, Figures, & Opinions

Leigh Clayborne

MASON CREST

Mason Crest
450 Parkway Drive, Suite D
Broomall, Pennsylvania 19008
(866) MCP-BOOK (toll-free)
www.masoncrest.com

First printing
9 8 7 6 5 4 3 2 1

ISBN (hardback) 978-1-4222-4106-6
ISBN (series) 978-1-4222-4103-5
ISBN (ebook) 978-1-4222-7694-5

Cataloging-in-Publication Data on file with the Library of Congress

NATIONAL HIGHLIGHTS

Developed and Produced by National Highlights Inc.
Editor: Andrew Morkes
Interior and cover design: Yolanda Van Cooten
Proofreader: Mika Jin
Production: Michelle Luke

QR CODES AND LINKS TO THIRD-PARTY CONTENT

contents

KEY ICONS TO LOOK FOR:

Words to understand: These words with their easy-to-understand definitions will increase the reader's understanding of the text while building vocabulary skills.

Sidebars: This boxed material within the main text allows readers to build knowledge, gain insights, explore possibilities, and broaden their perspectives by weaving together additional information to provide realistic and holistic perspectives.

Educational Videos: Readers can view videos by scanning our QR codes, providing them with additional educational content to supplement the text. Examples include news coverage, moments in history, speeches, iconic sports moments and much more!

Text-dependent questions: These questions send the reader back to the text for more careful attention to the evidence presented there.

Research projects: Readers are pointed toward areas of further inquiry connected to each chapter. Suggestions are provided for projects that encourage deeper research and analysis.

Series glossary of key terms: This back-of-the-book glossary contains terminology used throughout this series. Words found here increase the reader's ability to read and comprehend higher-level books and articles in this field.

Introduction

It often takes decades, or even a lifetime, for major changes in public opinion to occur. For example, it took until 1920 for the U.S. Congress to grant women across the country the right to vote—more than 140 years after the U.S. was founded. But in the case of marijuana, public opinion seems to have changed much faster. Over the past two decades or so, its usage has been decriminalized or legalized, normalized, and even celebrated in some countries and U.S. states.

Once a taboo topic, now many regular people—and celebrities—aren't afraid to say that they use it. Many support its legalization. From singers Lady Gaga and Rhianna, to actor Morgan Freeman, to U.S. Senator Rand Paul, people are showing their support. But some people still oppose marijuana usage. They see it as a dangerous drug. U.S. Attorney General Jeff Sessions, Pope Francis, and other notable public figures have spoken out against it for various reasons.

Depending on which "side" you're on, you may want to demonize those who disagree with you (which you should never do). But the fact is that it's not a simple issue. Both sides make some very good points, as we'll discuss in this book. We'll look at the arguments, opinions, and research shaping this controversial issue.

The State of Public Opinion

What percentage of people think that marijuana should be legal in the U.S. compared to last year? Ten years ago? Fifty years ago? Let's take a look.

The Pew Research Center is an organization of trusted experts who study a variety of issues. They gather data, analyze it, and provide summaries of this information in the form of statistics and research reports. According to its research, as of 2016, more than half (57 percent) of adults in the U.S. believed that marijuana should be legal. This is in stark contrast to just ten years ago, when only 32 percent held this opinion. Among teens like you, the opinion that it should be legal in the U.S. is up to an astounding 71 percent. In 2006, only 34 percent of teens favored legalization.

Gallup, a respected polling organization, conducted a survey in late 2017. Its findings were similar to those of the Pew Research Center. The Gallup poll showed, just one year later, that 64 percent of people favored legalization in the United States. Gallup points out that only 12 percent of people held this opinion in 1969, when your grandparents were close to your age.

The State of Legalization

In Canada, marijuana usage for any reason is legal as of July 2018. But, just like alcohol and cigarettes, age-verification is required. Many other countries also have

Oregon's Finest - Chocolate Melt

Strain Facts

THC..............73.58%
CBD..............1.78%
CBN..............4.39%

Test Date 8-24-12
Tracking# 101732

Oregon's Finest - God/Lemon Wax

Strain Facts

THC..............87.23%
CBD..............1.02%
CBN..............2.20%

Test Date 8-24-12
Tracking# 101725

Hybrid
Bry
Blueberry

Liberty Farms
"Blueberry"
Use For: Pain Relief,
Stress, Anxiety

NOT FOR SALE
Medical Use Only
ORS 475.300-475.346

Hybrid
Che
Chernobyl

Heavenly Herbs
"Chernobyl"
Use for: Pain Relief,
Nausea, Stress

NOT FOR SALE
Medical Use Only
ORS 475.300-475.346

Mg

Heavenly Herbs
"Mean Green"
Use For: Pain Relief,
Nausea, Stress

NOT FOR SALE
Medical Use Only
ORS 475.300-475.346

Hybrid
Atn

Liberty Farms
"ATN"
Use For: Pain Relief, THC,
Stress, Migraines

NOT FOR SALE
Medical Use Only
ORS 475.300-475.346

legalized either medical or recreational usage. Around the world, from Israel to Uruguay, governments have opted for some form of legalization.

Marijuana has been decriminalized in many U.S. states, but it's still illegal at the national level (as of the writing of this book). Decriminalization means that something is technically still illegal, but the government has decided to reduce or eliminate penalties up to a certain limit.

Legalization or decriminalization are growing trends that are picking up steam. Yet, the U.S. federal government and many other countries still officially consider marijuana a dangerous and illegal drug. Will this change soon? What do you think?

In this book, we'll explore where legalization of marijuana stands today around the world and what various public figures, medical associations and other organizations, and governments think about legalization.

The State of Medical Research

As public opinion shifts and laws around the world loosen, there are more opportunities to conduct research. Scientists now have better access to marijuana samples that were previously illegal to possess. And they can test marijuana on willing human participants. Researchers need to study both the benefits—and the side effects—of marijuana.

Long-term studies in clinical settings are needed to confirm the medicinal qualities of marijuana. But, in the short term, there are many promising studies that demonstrate the healing potential for medical marijuana. They show that it can effectively reduce symptoms in people with all kinds of conditions. People with everything from seizures to post-traumatic stress disorder may benefit. We'll take a closer look at some of these studies. We'll look at the medical research that supports using marijuana to help with many illnesses and the side effects of cancer treatments. We'll also consider what's happening in the recreational market. Finally, we'll evaluate what's happened in the past twenty years to push this issue to the forefront, and we'll imagine what the future of marijuana may be based on what has happened so far. So, let's get started.

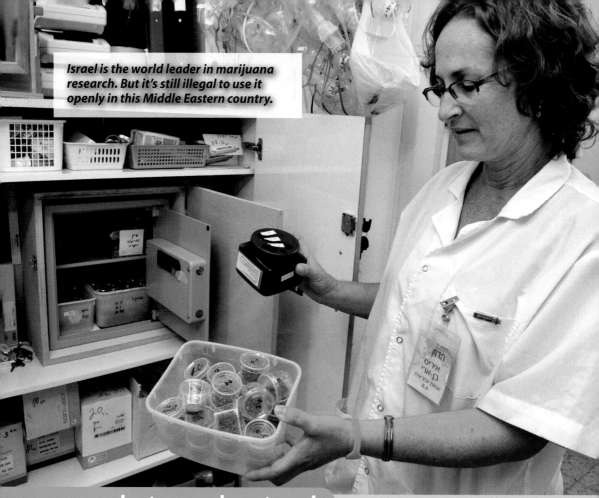

Israel is the world leader in marijuana research. But it's still illegal to use it openly in this Middle Eastern country.

words to understand

bill: A document written by elected officials to propose a new law. It must be voted on and passed by a group of elected officials before it becomes law.

cannabis: A plant whose flowers are dried and turned into marijuana.

decriminalization: Means that something is technically still illegal, but the government has decided to reduce or get rid of penalties up to a certain limit.

parliament: A group of people in India, the United Kingdom, and other countries who are elected by citizens of that particular country to determine the laws of the land. In the U.S., this group is called Congress.

recreational use: Using marijuana for anything other than to treat a medical problem.

chapter 1

Views of Marijuana Around the World

A person's views are normally shaped by the people around them. You may believe some things because your parents do. Other opinions may be shaped by your teachers, friends, or what you see on television or on a news website.

If you live in the United States, Canada, India, or another country, it's easy to only think about an issue based on your own country's views. But in order to better understand where marijuana stands today, it's important to look around the world. Having more global insight not only helps you better understand the issues at hand, but also helps you predict what may happen in your own country down the road and learn about different points of view.

Let's take a look.

India

In India, the use of marijuana is technically illegal. Some provinces in India tolerate it much like some states do the same in the United States. Approximately 80 percent of people in India practice the religion of Hinduism. This fact makes it difficult for the country to completely reject marijuana. Marijuana usage is deeply rooted in some Hindu practices. It's used to both enhance spiritual experiences and as a treatment for many conditions. Ancient texts dating back to 2000 B.C. even refer to **cannabis** as one of five sacred plants said to have "magical properties." The government regulates marijuana and permits its sale in various forms in some temples. But outside of religious practice, the use of marijuana is illegal.

Wild & Free

Marijuana is native to India. This means that it grew naturally there before people began growing it as a crop for medicinal and recreational use. This contrasts with places like the United States and Canada, where marijuana doesn't naturally grow. It must be farmed and cared for. If you find a field of marijuana in a U.S. forest, you can be certain that someone planted it there.

There is a small, but growing, movement to legalize marijuana in India across its provinces. In late 2017, a **bill** was introduced to India's **parliament** to distinguish marijuana from harder drugs like opium or cocaine. If this bill passes, it would remove the current penalties and put systems in place to regulate both medical and **recreational use**.

China

In China, the possession and sale of marijuana is technically illegal. But the enforcement of these laws is somewhat lax. While people don't openly share that they use marijuana, they may do so in secret—taking precautions not to get noticed by law enforcement.

In China, on the whole, using drugs is considered dishonorable. In a culture where honor is important, cities and communities may continue to call it illegal "on the books" to maintain their honor. But at the same time, they often turn a blind eye if people who sell and use it are discreet. In cases where low-level drug offenders are prosecuted (punished), mandatory drug rehabilitation is the most common penalty. In fact, by many accounts, smoking marijuana openly is really not that big of a deal as long as a person doesn't walk around saying, "I'm smoking illegal drugs."

China's system may seem contradictory (not logical) to an outsider. But it seems to work for them. There are currently no open talks in China about legalizing marijuana in the future.

Israel

Many of the studies that people use to support the benefits of marijuana didn't come from the western world. They come from Israel, in the Middle East, where scientists are actively studying marijuana benefits and side effects.

However, if someone gets caught using marijuana outside of their home or without a permit in Israel, they could face a hefty fine. And there's currently a four-strike policy, so getting caught breaking the law a fourth time could result in a person receiving a more serious penalty. Israeli law doesn't currently distinguish between marijuana and harder drugs when it comes to recreational use.

According to the *Jerusalem Post*, a 2014 poll showed that around 43 percent of college-age students believed that marijuana should be decriminalized and regulated for recreational use. The support for legalization grows every year. But only 2 percent think that recreational marijuana should be a "free for all." This public opinion is reflected in current law. Will it change in the near future? We'll have to wait and see.

Saudi Arabia

We've thus far discussed some countries where marijuana usage is taken very lightly even if it's technically illegal. Let's look at a country that goes in the other direction.

DrugAbuse.com lists Saudi Arabia as among the strictest countries in the world when it comes to penalties for drug selling and use. Marijuana and alcohol are both illegal there.

If someone is caught, they might face:

- Ten years in prison
- Heavy fines
- 150 lashes with a whip/flog
- The death penalty (for a severe offense such as drug smuggling)

Other countries with severe penalties include:

- North Korea
- Costa Rica

- Indonesia
- Colombia
- Iran

In these countries, prison sentences of greater than ten years and a fine of U.S. $30,000 or more are not uncommon. If someone is caught possessing or selling large amounts of marijuana, they could face life in prison or a death sentence. If a tourist is caught bringing drugs into North Korea, for example, he or she may be sentenced to many years in a hard-labor prison camp. Many people don't survive their sentences.

Zimbabwe

As it stands now, a person in Zimbabwe could face twelve years in prison if convicted of using marijuana. But this may soon change. This country in southern Africa is considering following the lead of many other African countries in legalizing marijuana for medical use.

Advocates see marijuana as an opportunity to bring new foreign investment into the country. Helen Jackson, the author of *AIDS Africa: Continent in Crisis*, points out that:

"Most recreational drugs are illegal. Marijuana needs special consideration. Although excessive use should be avoided, marijuana aids relaxation, acts as an anti-con-vulsant [stops or reduces the frequency of seizures], reduces nausea, and promotes a sense of well-being. It also stimulates appetite and thereby assists weight gain."

Much-Needed Relief

The United Nations estimates that in the African country of Zimbabwe, nearly two million people over the age of fifteen are living with HIV/AIDs. This incurable and deadly disease causes dangerous weight loss, nausea, and lack of desire to eat, among other symptoms. Advocates of medical marijuana legalization see it as much-needed relief to this suffering.

All About Hashish

Hashish is a thick, sticky resin derived from the cannabis plant that also produces marijuana. It's commonly smoked in India and was introduced to South Africa by Indian migrant workers in 1860.

Morocco and Afghanistan are major producers of hashish.

The United Nations estimates that around 15 percent of the thirteen million people in Zimbabwe are living with HIV or AIDs. Like many other advocates in the region, Ms. Jackson sees marijuana as a much-needed remedy for the suffering of those with AIDS.

Ethiopia

Ethiopia is in east-central Africa. In this country, marijuana use is illegal, and people receive stiff penalties if they are caught using or selling it. However, because Ethiopia is largely rural and agricultural, many communities grow marijuana in secluded locations and share it only among family and friends to avoid interference from law enforcement.

Netherlands

While many countries move toward legalization of marijuana, the Netherlands has been there for more than forty years. You could consider this country a pioneer in legalization. But its laws have changed dramatically over the years as it seeks to balance public demand with public safety.

In 1972, this European country made the possession of small amounts of marijuana a lesser crime than possessing other more harmful drugs. In 1976, it allowed coffee shops to sell marijuana in small amounts to their patrons. Possession elsewhere continued to be illegal. In 2003, medical marijuana became legal.

Oddly, it's still illegal to grow marijuana and sell marijuana in large quantities to the coffee shops. But this is changing. According to the *Washington Post*, 65 percent of Dutch residents (the people of the Netherlands) think that marijuana production and usage should be completely legalized. Fifty-seven percent feel that they should be allowed to grow their own plants.

But there's another side to this. You may have heard of Amsterdam. That's a city in the Netherlands famous around the world for its coffee shops. This city has recently had to crack down on usage by tourists who were flocking to the city and causing a public nuisance. Opponents of further **decriminalization** and legalization are concerned that Amsterdam will continue to be a tourist magnet for people who want to visit for no other reason than to get high.

The Netherlands has been a pioneer in marijuana legalization. Above, a coffee shop in the Red Light District in Amsterdam, Netherlands.

THE HISTORY OF MARIJUANA IN AMSTERDAM

Learn about the history of marijuana in Amsterdam:

Denmark

In Denmark, recreational use is against the law. But the government of this small country in northern Europe does allow certain approved medications that are derived from the cannabis plant. Historically, recreational use has been tolerated in its capital, Copenhagen. According to TripAdvisor.com, the "hippie district" of Christiana in Copenhagen is the place where locals can buy marijuana openly. Possession of small quantities is technically still illegal and may result in fines. Possessing larger amounts could land a person in jail.

Spain

Spain is now considered one of the most marijuana-friendly places in Europe. Laws are determined regionally so marijuana usage rules vary depending on where a person is in the country. In Catalonia (a region of Spain), enforcement is particularly lax with marijuana clubs found throughout its cities. In other places, like the capital of Madrid, usage is less open. The Canna Law Group, a marijuana business advocacy organization, estimates that 10 percent of the adult population in Spain uses marijuana in some form.

United Kingdom

Marijuana is still illegal in the United Kingdom, which includes the countries of:

- England
- Wales
- Scotland
- Northern Ireland

Even though it's technically illegal, *The Sun* reports that some police forces only loosely enforce marijuana laws. This more laid-back approach to law enforcement means that people who know when and where it's usage is "okay," won't typically be fined. This is similar to China's policy where if a person is discreet, they're unlikely to be arrested for possessing small amounts in areas of the United Kingdom where the police force takes this stance on enforcement. However, if a neighbor reports a person for selling or using marijuana, the police force is said to be more likely to enforce the law.

Changing Views of Marijuana by the U.K. Government?

According to the Home Office (a government department) in the United Kingdom (UK), "it remains illegal for UK residents to possess cannabis in any form." But views of medical marijuana may be changing. The government's Medicines and Healthcare Products Regulatory Agency has confirmed that cannabidiol has a "restoring, correcting, or modifying" effect on "physiological functions" when given to people. Cannabidiol is a chemical compound found in the cannabis plant that is non-psychoactive. It is known for its medicinal and pain relief properties.

In 2014, Uruguay legalized both recreational and medical marijuana.

Uruguay

This South American country decided to fight fire with fire. For decades, Uruguay was threatened by a significant illegal drug trade. This drug trade led to violence and death. After spending many years and resources trying to arrest drug growers and dealers, in 2014 Uruguay made marijuana legal and available for purchase in local pharmacies with a government-issued identification card. This made Uruguay the first country in the world where marijuana is 100 percent legal.

Its goal is to put the illegal drug dealers out of business by making it easier and cheaper for people to get marijuana legally. Government officials also hope to reduce the manufacture and sale of more harmful drugs such as cocaine because people have a "safer" alternative.

Brazil

Brazil decriminalized the growing and selling, as well as the possession of small amounts of marijuana more than ten years ago. In 2017, this South American country issued its first license to sell medicine made from cannabis. Several patients exercised their legal rights in the court system to get the laws changed. And thanks to this new law, obtaining a cannabis-based treatment is 100 percent legal.

Australia

In January 2018, Australia legalized the export of medical marijuana to other countries. It expects this change to boost the economy significantly. Niv Dagan, a director at investment firm PEAK Asset Management told a CNN reporter, [This] "opens the floodgates for further overseas investment into Australia." He estimates that the Australian medical marijuana market could exceed U.S. $1 billion by 2020.

This is astounding considering that medical marijuana was only legalized in the country two years before. Growing, selling, and having medical marijuana is legal in Australia if a person follows the related laws. Recreational use, however, is still illegal.

"There is no doubt that the primary concern of policing in Canada is impaired driving. It is our belief that it will become an even greater issue with the legalization of cannabis."

–Mario Harel, director of the Gatineau (Quebec) Police Service, in 2017 testimony to the House of Commons Justice Committee

In 2018, Australia legalized the export of medical marijuana to other countries. Recreational marijuana is still illegal.

Canada

According to a poll by the Angus Reid Institute, two-thirds of Canadians think that marijuana should be completely legal in the country. On July 1, 2018, Canada Day, marijuana for both medical and recreational use will become legal—unless authorities decide to take some more time to prepare for this big move. Each province will determine the legal age at which someone can buy marijuana.

Despite this move toward legalization, surveys show that more than 50 percent of the country is hesitant. They think that the legalization date should be delayed. Their primary concern is that the infrastructure (including training for police) needed for national legalization isn't in place. They feel that this could lead to confusion and chaos.

United States

In the United States, marijuana is legal in some form in more than half of its states. States such as Arizona and North Dakota have chosen to legalize it for medical use only. In states such as Maine and Colorado, they've opted to legalize both medical and recreational use. Some states, such as Mississippi and Alabama, permit medical use on a very limited, case-by-case basis. These states aren't typically included among lists of states where marijuana is legal because the approval is so restrictive.

It's illegal in the United States for a doctor to write a prescription for marijuana because at the national level it's still illegal. Doctors may only write a recommendation letter for patients who they feel may benefit from using marijuana. Also, because it's illegal nationally, people may not take marijuana across state lines or carry it with them while traveling on a commercial airplane.

States that have not legalized the use of marijuana hope to wait and see how legalization impacts other states first. In some states, such as Mississippi, there just isn't enough public support for legalization. Even though some polls show 60 percent of Mississippians support legalization, advocacy groups haven't been able to get enough support to get the laws changed.

Political Battles Continue in the U.S. Regarding Marijuana

Through 2016, the federal government had taken a hands-off approach when it came to marijuana legalization. It allowed states to devise their own laws regarding the legalization of marijuana—even though it was still illegal at the federal level. This began to change when the Trump Administration came to power. In 2018, Attorney General Jeff Sessions, a fierce opponent of marijuana legalization, rescinded three memos from the Obama Administration, which had adopted a policy of non-interference with marijuana-friendly state laws. In a written statement, he called the shift a "return to the rule of law." He also said in a memo to all federal prosecutors: "These principles require federal prosecutors deciding which cases to prosecute to weigh all relevant considerations of the crime, the deterrent effect of criminal prosecution, and the cumulative impact of particular crimes on the community."

The actions of Sessions angered many Democrats and some Republicans (especially those representing states where marijuana is legal). Here are some responses from members of Congress and the legal marijuana industry to Sessions' actions:

"I will be putting a hold on every single nomination from the Department of Justice until Attorney General Jeff Sessions lives up to the commitment he made to me in my pre-confirmation meeting with him. The conversation we had that was specifically about this issue of states' rights in Colorado. The people of Colorado deserve answers. The people of Colorado deserve to be respected."

—Republic Senator Cory Gardner of Colorado

"Trump promised to let states set their own marijuana policies. Now he's breaking that promise so Jeff Sessions can pursue his extremist anti-marijuana crusade. Once again the Trump administration is doubling down on protecting states' rights only when they believe the state is right."

—Democratic Senator, Ron Wyden of Oregon

"I expect any actions he and the Justice Department take against the industry will be met with significant pushback from states that are benefiting greatly from an economic and quality of life standpoint. The cannabis industry will continue on regardless of this decision, and in the long run this should only be a roadblock."

—Jeffrey Zucker, president of Green Lion Partners, a Denver firm that promotes marijuana businesses, in *POLITICO Magazine*

U.S. Congresswoman Barbara Lee of California strongly opposes U.S. Attorney General Jeff Sessions' attempts to strengthen anti-marijuana laws. In a conference call to reporters, Lee said, "As a person of color, let me just say that the War on Drugs has been a failure... We've lost families, we've lost a generation. So this affects people of color in a big way, so we're not going to allow them to turn back the clock. In our district, we're going to fight this every step of the way."

text-dependent questions

1. In India, the government has had trouble making marijuana completely illegal because of its ties to what major religion?

2. In Zimbabwe, advocates hope that medical marijuana will help patients suffering from what disease plaguing the country?

3. In Uruguay, the government has legalized and regulated marijuana in an effort to do what?

research project

Choose a country that interests you. Collect additional resources online to learn more about how that country regulates marijuana. Write a two-page paper that explores the topic.

The singer Rihanna openly supports marijuana legalization, but acknowledges that marijuana can negatively affect frequent users.

words to understand

advocate: Someone who supports something openly.

opioids: Highly addictive prescription and non-prescription painkillers. They are often sold, obtained, and used illegally. Overdose deaths are common.

opponent: Someone who is against something.

propaganda: Intentionally misleading information put out by an organization such as a government, religious group, or news source. Its goal is to convince people to have a certain opinion that they might not have if they knew the truth.

proposition: A part of the U.S. democratic system that allows voters to vote on whether something should become a new law. Also abbreviated as **prop.**

chapter 2

Marijuana Advocates and Opponents

While it's easy to oversimplify an issue by calling some people **advocates** and others **opponents**, the truth is usually more mixed. Sometimes people are okay with certain aspects of an issue. But they have concerns. Still others have no opinion about an issue.

In this chapter, we'll look at where various celebrities, politicians, and business people stand on marijuana legalization. We'll hear them discuss their beliefs. We'll look at actions that they've taken to either support or oppose marijuana legalization.

Danny DeVito

Danny DeVito is an Emmy Award–winning actor whose most recent claim to fame is his work on the TV show It's *Always Sunny in Philadelphia*. He is an avid supporter of legalizing marijuana. DeVito has been quoted as saying that he's "very excited about legalization." He has openly discussed using marijuana with other actors.

In 2010, Californians had the opportunity to vote on **Proposition** 19 at the polls. DeVito encouraged his fellow Californians to get out and vote for the proposition. This proposition would effectively make it legal to grow, possess, transport, and sell marijuana for recreational use. Prop 19 was narrowly defeated. But in November 2016, Californians got another chance with Prop 64. Fifty-seven percent of Californians who cast a ballot voted to legalize and regulate recreational marijuana in the state.

According to the *New York Times*, retail marijuana shops opened their doors for the first time in California in December 2017. Prior to this law's passage, only medical marijuana was legal in California.

Rihanna

Rihanna openly supports marijuana legalization. The outspoken singer hasn't been shy about posting photographs on social media. In them, she is often smoking marijuana recreationally. While she has been a vocal advocate, she has more recently stated that she has cut back on her usage. While she enjoys using marijuana, she realizes that overdoing it isn't good for her health. Rihanna recognizes that putting any mind-altering substance into her body can have long-term effects on it.

Miley Cyrus

Former Disney star and singer Miley Cyrus told *Rolling Stone* that marijuana was "the best drug on earth" in a 2013 interview. In 2014 at a London concert, she expressed her views that it should be legalized. But fast forward to 2017, when Cyrus stated that she had quit using marijuana completely. Her reasons for quitting included her desires to be around more positive people and think more clearly. Like Rihanna, Cyrus' move to give up marijuana shows that she understands something very important about any type of drug. If something impacts your life negatively, it's become an addiction that you're better off without.

"I like to surround myself with people that make me want to get better, more evolved, open. And I was noticing it's not the people that are stoned. I want to be super clear and sharp, because I know exactly where I want to be."

—**Miley Cyrus, Singer, *Billboard*, 2017**

Other celebrities who once advocated for marijuana and later chose to give it up include:

- Woody Harrelson, actor
- James Franco, actor
- André 3000, actor, singer/songwriter
- Lady Gaga, singer/actress
- Brad Pitt, actor
- Mark Wahlberg, actor

Their reasons vary, but are very similar to those of Miley Cyrus and Rihanna.

"I am a party animal. But on the other hand, I'm now extremely moderate, and ... I actually stopped smoking pot almost a year ago.... I feel like it was keeping me from being emotionally available."

—**Woody Harrelson, actor, in an interview in *Vulture*, 2017**

Megan Fox

Actress Megan Fox calls the United States' stance on marijuana "all **propaganda**." She openly supports legalization and considers it "not a big deal." She expressed her view in an interview with British GQ:

"I can't tell you how much ... I've been through because I will openly say that I smoke weed...People look at it like it's this crazy, hippy ... thing to do. And it's not!"

Morgan Freeman

Actor Morgan Freeman states that marijuana helps treat his fibromyalgia. That's a painful muscle and bone condition. Freeman believes that it should be legalized everywhere for both medical and recreational use.

The actress Megan Fox believes that the use of marijuana is "not a big deal."

"I have fibromyalgia pain in this arm, and the only thing that offers any relief is marijuana. They're talking about kids who have grand mal seizures, and they've discovered that marijuana eases that down to where these children can have a life. That right there, to me, says, 'Legalize it across the board!'"

—Morgan Freeman, Academy Award–winning actor, *Daily Beast*

Dalai Lama

The Tibetan spiritual leader known as the Dalai Lama spoke with TIME in 2014. When asked if he supports medical marijuana, he gave a somewhat mixed response.

"No. Never. These kinds of substances are generally considered poison, very bad. But for particular illnesses, this is sometimes deliberately used. So that's up to the doctor, or up to scientists. The ability to judge reality is something very unique. Our brain is something very special. So if that is damaged, that's awful. So alcohol and drugs are very bad."

What do you take from his statement? One could argue that he does recognize that marijuana does have some harmful side effects. If one can avoid it, they should because it's healthier to do so. But it appears that he does agree that like many drugs that have side effects, sometimes it's needed. Ultimately, the Dalai Lama believes that a doctor should make that call.

Bernie Sanders

Vermont Senator Bernie Sanders supports legalization of medical marijuana. He also supports decriminalization of recreational marijuana. Sanders believes that the U.S. federal government should lift its national marijuana ban and allow each state to decide. He is a strong advocate for getting people help if they're addicted rather than treating those who abuse drugs like criminals.

"Marijuana is not the same as heroin. No one who has seriously studied the issue believes that marijuana should be classified as a Schedule 1 drug beside killer drugs like heroin. Quite the contrary. We should allow states the right to move toward the decriminalization of marijuana, not reverse the progress that has been made in recent years."

—Bernie Sanders, U.S. Senator, at his website

U.S. Senator Bernie Sanders supports legalization of medical marijuana and the decriminalization of recreational marijuana.

Elizabeth Warren

Massachusetts Senator Elizabeth Warren would like to see marijuana used to fight the opioid epidemic in the United States. **Opioids** are very powerful and addictive prescription and non-prescription painkillers. Drug overdoses (including those from opioids) killed more than 64,000 people in the United States in 2016, according to the Centers for Disease Control.

U.S. Senator Elizabeth Warren wants marijuana to be used to fight the opioid epidemic in the United States.

In the *Journal of the American Medical Association*, one can find studies that have shown that marijuana can effectively treat pain. Senator Warren believes that if patients had legal access to marijuana, fewer people would turn to these dangerous prescription and illegal drugs.

Studies support her statements. One such study published in *Drug and Alcohol Review* shows that as many as 80 percent of people who use marijuana prefer it to taking opioids. Opioids cause dizziness, nausea, severe drowsiness, trouble breathing, and physical dependence. Marijuana has fewer side effects than opium. If given the option to use a drug that has fewer side effects, people take that option.

"Opioid abuse is a national concern and warrants swift and immediate action....Medical marijuana has the potential to mitigate the effects of the opioid crisis."

—Elizabeth Warren, U.S. Senator, from Warren's website and from a letter to Alex Azar, President Trump's nominee to lead the U.S. Department of Health and Human Services

Peter Thiel

Peter Thiel, the founder of PayPal, is betting his money on the future of marijuana. He actively invests in marijuana-related companies. He sees bright days ahead for the industry and wants to be a part of its growth and expansion. As an investor, he gives money to innovative marijuana companies in exchange for owning a percentage of their company. If the companies profit, so does he.

Rand Paul

Kentucky Senator Rand Paul believes that each state should be able to decide how marijuana is treated in that state. He feels that the U.S. federal government should stay out of it. If people are struggling with addiction, Paul believes that they should receive treatment rather than prison. Senator Paul has stated that he doesn't think that marijuana use should be encouraged because it does have negative side effects. But he doesn't think people should be jailed—potentially destroying their lives—for using or selling marijuana.

"I think putting somebody in jail for ten years for possession of marijuana or sale of marijuana is ridiculous."

—Rand Paul, U.S. Senator, in an interview on *Face the Nation*, 2014

Richard Branson

Billionaire businessman Richard Branson shares Elizabeth Warren's view that marijuana legalization could be an important tool to help manage the opioid crisis in the United States. Like Senator Paul and others, he thinks we should help people who are addicted and stop criminalizing them. Legalizing and regulating it is the way to go in his mind.

Businessman Richard Branson believes that marijuana should be decriminalized and regulated.

"What the U.S. doesn't need is another frontline in the War on Drugs. Decriminalization, regulation, and harm reduction are the way to go. Everything else will cost lives and money."

—Richard Branson, founder of the Virgin Group, which controls more than 400 companies, on Twitter (@richardbranson)

George Zimmer

George Zimmer, the founder of Men's Warehouse and a serial-entrepreneur, has never been shy about speaking on controversial issues. He says that marijuana helped change the course of his life. Zimmer has recounted his days as an alcoholic and how "switching one addiction for another" helped him become alcohol free.

He doesn't glorify marijuana. But he does consider it "harm reduction." He told Business Insider: "The fact is—and I mean the scientific fact—[marijuana] is less toxic and dangerous than cigarettes and alcohol, which are the main drugs in the United States." Zimmer donated $50,000 to help fund efforts to get recreational marijuana legalized, according to *Fortune*.

George Soros

Billionaire activist George Soros is another businessman betting on marijuana in the United States. He worked with companies to raise $16 million to help get the word out about Prop 64. That's the California proposition that finally legalized recreational marijuana in California. He has been involved with legalization efforts in almost every state, as well as the country of Uruguay. George Soros sees marijuana as a huge business opportunity. He's investing in companies and people who are on the cutting-edge of the industry.

"Our marijuana laws are clearly doing more harm than good."
—George Soros, billionaire activist in an op-ed in the Wall Street Journal in 2010

Rahm Emanuel

Like many of the people we've discussed thus far, Chicago Mayor Rahm Emanuel's position on marijuana isn't one-sided. He supported an ordinance (rules) that reduced penalties for possession of small amounts of marijuana, as well as other recreational drugs. His stated reasoning was to free up the city's police force to handle more serious crimes.

Then, in 2014, the *Chicago Tribune* reported that Mayor Emanuel rejected the idea that Chicago should legalize and tax marijuana stating that he doesn't "think you should balance the budget by promoting recreational smoking of pot." His opponents pointed out that Colorado had raised as much as $21.6 million in taxes and fees since legalizing recreational marijuana in the state the year before. Like many, Mayor Emanuel is hesitant to support full legalization because marijuana does have harmful side effects.

Through 2018, Chicago is conducting a medical marijuana pilot program. The results of the program will be analyzed to determine if Chicago will continue to allow medical marijuana. If approved, recreational marijuana may be the logical next step. But it's too early to say for sure.

Changes in Law Enforcement Tactics

Chicago Mayor Rahm Emanuel believes that allowing police officers to ticket, rather than arrest, low-level drug offenders could save his city more than $1 million a year. He told the Chicago City Council: "It's not just about saving taxpayer dollars, it's also about saving nonviolent offenders from a lifetime spent in and out of the criminal justice system. A felony conviction can slam the door on someone's future and make it harder to go to school, apply for financial aid, and find housing. There are times when a felony conviction is no doubt warranted, but we have to ask ourselves whether it's too high a price for using drugs."

Chicago mayor Rahm Emmanuel has advocated for the decriminalization of marijuana to allow police to address more serious crimes.

Find out about Mayor Rahm Emanuel's stance on decriminalization in this news story:

Pope Francis

Pope Francis is not in favor of drug legalization. During a visit to St. Francis of Assisi of the Providence of God Hospital in Rio de Janeiro in 2013 he said the following:

"A reduction in the spread and influence of drug addiction will not be achieved by a liberalization of drug use…Rather, it is necessary to confront the problems underlying the use of these drugs, by promoting greater justice, educating young people in the values that build up life in society, accompanying those in difficulty, and giving them hope for the future."

Pope Francis sees marijuana usage as a symptom of societal and personal issues. From his statement, we can conclude that he thinks we should be looking at what's causing someone to want to use marijuana rather than legalizing it. He believes that if society addresses injustice and gives people hope, fewer people will want to use drugs like marijuana.

Pope Francis sees marijuana usage as a symptom of societal and personal issues.

"I reject the idea that America will be a better place if marijuana is sold in every corner store. And I am astonished to hear people suggest that we can solve our heroin crisis by legalizing marijuana—so people can trade one life-wrecking dependency for another that's only slightly less awful. Our nation needs to say clearly once again that using drugs will destroy your life."

—Jeff Sessions, U.S. Attorney General, 2017

Jeff Sessions

Jeff Sessions is the U.S. Attorney General. That makes him the head of the U.S. Department of Justice (DOJ). The DOJ is a part of the executive branch of the U.S. government. This branch of government, which also includes the President of the United States, is responsible for enforcing federal laws. As such, regardless of his own views, he's responsible for ensuring that federal laws are followed.

He's the one person in this list of advocates and opponents who has legal power to directly influence federal decisions related to marijuana. Regardless of whether he speaks his own views or is speaking on behalf of the federal government, Sessions has been consistently opposed to marijuana. He doesn't distinguish between medical use and recreational use.

This twelve-year-ol girl who uses mari-juana to control her seizures is suing Jef Sessions and the Dr Enforcement Agenc to legalize the use o medical marijuana across the country.

Marijuana is a unique case. While it's illegal at the national level, some could argue that the U.S. Constitution doesn't give the federal government the authority to regulate marijuana. According to the U.S. Constitution, the states have the say on most things that go on in their state.

"The powers not delegated to the United States by the Constitution, nor prohibited by it to the states, are reserved to the States respectively, or to the people."

—Tenth Amendment of the U.S. Constitution

However, this has been challenged again and again on many issues.

In January 2018, Attorney General Sessions authorized a "crackdown" on marijuana possession in states that have legalized or decriminalized it. He admits that the federal government has limited resources to prosecute offenders in a January 2018 statement to the press.

In deciding which marijuana activities to prosecute under these laws with the department's finite resources, prosecutors should follow the well-established principles that govern all federal prosecutions…These principles require federal prosecutors deciding which cases to prosecute to weigh all relevant considerations of the crime, the deterrent effect of criminal prosecution, and the cumulative impact of particular crimes on the community.

In other words, he states that the courts should only take cases that can have a great impact on the industry. He wants to make others think twice about growing, selling, and possessing marijuana. As of the writing of this book, this is a developing story, so the outcome is unclear. This simply demonstrates how fast-changing and controversial this issue is.

text-dependent questions

1. What reason did Rihanna give for choosing to reduce her marijuana usage?
2. What reason did Senator Elizabeth Warren give for supporting the legalization of medical marijuana?
3. What does Pope Francis feel we should address instead of legalizing marijuana?

research project

Gather additional resources and write a two-page argumentative essay in which you evaluate the arguments and evidence and establish a position on the issue of marijuana legalization.

It is legal to use medical marijuana in the majority of U.S. states and more than twenty other countries.

words to understand

chronic pain: Pain that won't go away and that interferes with daily life.

disability claim: A request by a person to a government to provide financial support due to his or her inability to work because of a disability.

intelligence quotient: The level of someone's intelligence as determined by a standardized test.

paranoia: An irrational fear that causes a person to think that someone or something is trying to hurt them.

chapter 3

Medical Marijuana

What is medical marijuana? Is there real proof that it can help treat the symptoms of severe medical conditions? How do doctors feel about medical marijuana? Are there any side effects? There are many important questions to ask when considering the topic of medical marijuana. For many, the idea of medical marijuana and recreational marijuana are very different. Many see medical marijuana as okay. But they don't think that it should be widely available for recreational use because of its side effects. In this chapter, we'll look at the facts, figures, studies, and opinions related to medical marijuana usage and perceptions. We'll explore the answers to these questions and more as we take a closer look at medical marijuana.

Medical Marijuana Use in the United States

Approximately two million people in the U.S. were registered as medical marijuana patients in 2017, according to Statista.com. California had the highest number of registered patients at more than 1.5 million. California also has more people than any other state in the U.S., which can help explain why the numbers are so high. Roughly 12 percent of the entire U.S. population lives in California, according to the U.S. Census Bureau. It's important to note that the number of people using medical marijuana regularly may be much lower. For example, in Colorado, another state where medical marijuana is legal, only 5 percent of registered patients get marijuana in a given month, according to state records.

A 2017 Gallup poll shows that 64 percent of people in the U.S. supported legalizing marijuana when not asked to distinguish between medical marijuana and recreational marijuana. A similar nationwide poll reported by the *Washington Times* in 2017 specifically asked about medical marijuana. This poll found that a staggering 86 percent of people in the U.S. supported marijuana for medical use. The same

California's Long Track Record of Legal Medical Marijuana

Medical marijuana has been legal in California since 1996. Lawmakers can study this long track record to decide if medical marijuana should become legal across the United States. According to the *Washington Post*, 92 percent of patients in California who use medical marijuana to treat a serious condition state that it helps reduce symptoms of their serious disorder. While this isn't scientific proof, it shows overwhelmingly that those using it believe they're getting the symptom relief they seek. The same study found another promising fact. It showed that despite legalization, only 5 percent of Californians use medical marijuana. This effectively dispels the myth that medical marijuana legalization increases the chance of abuse by people claiming to have health issues. As elected officials in the United States and other countries consider whether to legalize medical marijuana, they look to these examples to evaluate full legalization.

poll found that around 20 percent of people felt that we should have tougher laws regarding recreational use. It's important to realize that polls can vary, depending on their methods. No poll is 100 percent accurate. But repeated polls from trusted organizations show similar results and a clear trend. People in the U.S. overwhelmingly support full legalization of medical marijuana.

In the United States, more than one-hundred million people suffer from **chronic pain**, a type of pain that won't go away. For many, daily activities are excruciating and these individuals seek relief in whatever way possible. This has led many sufferers to turn to doctors who prescribe very strong and risky painkillers called opioids. These painkillers are highly addictive and can lead to illegal drug use. People either purchase more pills than they have been prescribed on the black market (a place where drugs and other goods are sold illegally). Or they turn to the illegal street drug heroin, which is also an opiate. Both scenarios are incredibly dangerous.

More than twenty-four million people worldwide abuse opioid drugs, according to the United Nations Office on Drugs and Crime. Around two million of these abusers are in the United States. The death rate from these drugs climbs year after year and is now reaching epidemic status. But one state, Colorado, saw a decline in opiate deaths by 6 percent in two years after marijuana became legal in the state, according to the National Institute on Drug Abuse. When given a choice between dangerous opiates and less harmful marijuana, people appear to choose marijuana to treat pain. More studies are needed to confirm this cause and effect scenario. But it's potentially yet another piece of evidence that will push toward nationwide legalization of medical marijuana.

Medical marijuana is also being used in conjunction with prescription opioids. Studies have also shown that inhaled marijuana has been found to complement prescription opioid pain medicines.

On the other side of the argument, there is some disturbing news. States that have approved the use of medical marijuana have seen a 24 percent increase in **disability claims** among people age twenty-four to forty years of age, according to a working paper from researchers at Temple University, Johns Hopkins University, and the University of Cincinnati. They're also seeing a 15 percent increase in work-related injury claims. No notable increases were seen in people age forty and over. The reasons for this increase have yet to be determined. A commonly stated mental side effect of marijuana usage is lack of motivation, so this definitely needs a closer look.

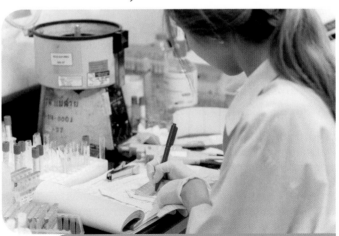

"Not only is medical marijuana effective for treating chronic and intractable pain, but inhaled marijuana has also been found to complement prescription opioid pain medicines well, enhancing the efficacy of (and safely interacting with) these more powerful narcotic medications and easing withdrawal symptoms."

—"Marijuana and Opiates," from the Drug Policy Alliance, 2016

Medical research continues to determine the positive and negative effects of marijuana.

What Science Shows

Supporters of medical marijuana claim that it can reduce the symptoms of many diseases. In some cases, there is strong evidence to support the benefits. In other cases, there is less evidence. In this section, we'll look at some of the conditions for which marijuana offers the most promising benefits.

Epilepsy

Epilepsy is a neurological disorder characterized by seizures. The sufferer may have them several times a day or week. During seizures, uncontrolled electrical signals pulse through the brain. The person loses complete control of the body and may convulse (shake violently). Someone with this condition may develop brain damage if the seizures aren't controlled. According to the Epilepsy Foundation, the results of studies of the use of marijuana to treat epilepsy have been very promising. It references one of the many studies that showed a 54 percent decrease in seizures for patients using a form of medical marijuana. Other people who have epilepsy and use medical marijuana, such as twelve-year-old Alexis Bortell, have not had a seizure since starting the treatment, according to CBS News. Alexis went from having seizures several times a week to not having one for two-plus years. Today, she strongly advocates for legalization. Many states in the U.S. that are against marijuana for any reason have special laws that allow it's use for epilepsy. The studies that show it's effective in treating epilepsy are that convincing. Many of these medical marijuana treatments, however, have the chemical THC removed. THC is the substance in marijuana that is known to cause mental side effects.

"Ever since I've been on this cannabis, I've actually been seizure-free for—today it's 974 days, so we're coming up on 1,000. So I think that's pretty good."

—Alexis Bortell, in a 2017 interview with CBS News

"The American Epilepsy Society (AES) calls on government and private funders to support well-designed clinical research into all promising treatments for epilepsy. To increase clinical research into the effectiveness and safety of marijuana as a possible treatment for resistant epilepsy, the AES urges that marijuana's status as a Federal Drug Enforcement Agency Schedule 1 controlled substance be reviewed. AES's call for rescheduling is not an endorsement of the legalization of marijuana, but is a recognition that the current restrictions on the use of medical marijuana for research continue to stand in the way of scientifically rigorous research into the development of cannabinoid-based treatments."

—2016 statement from the American Epilepsy Society at its website

Multiple Sclerosis

Multiple sclerosis is an immune system disorder that results in the immune system attacking its own nerve cells. Nerves send signals through the body telling different body parts what the brain wants them to do. And they send signals back to the brain, telling it what's happening to the body. Damaged nerves can't communicate effectively with the body. They may send false signals. This causes many symptoms,

Medical marijuana has been proven to help reduce the symptoms associated with multiple sclerosis, cancer, and other diseases.

including pain, numbness, paralysis, tremors, and violent muscle spasms. Studies have shown that medical marijuana may reduce the violent muscle spasms associated with multiple sclerosis, but it was less effective at treating tremors and other related symptoms. In one study, reported by the National Multiple Sclerosis Society, patients who were using medical marijuana were two times as likely to report that the muscle spasms had decreased when compared to those receiving a placebo. Another study showed that as many as 50 percent of people in the U.S. with multiple sclerosis are using marijuana to treat it even if they don't have a medical card that would allow them to legally do so.

"The question of whether marijuana…should be used for symptom management in multiple sclerosis (MS) is a complex one. It is generally agreed that better therapies are needed for distressing symptoms of MS—including pain, tremor and spasticity—that may not be sufficiently relieved by available treatments. Still, there are uncertainties about the benefits of marijuana relative to its side effects. The society supports the rights of people with MS to work with their MS health care providers to access marijuana for medical purposes in accordance with legal regulations in those states where such use has been approved. In addition, the society supports advancing research to better understand the benefits and potential risks of marijuana and its derivatives as a treatment for MS.

—2016 statement from the National Multiple Sclerosis Society at its website

Chronic Pain

Chronic pain is a type of pain that won't go away even when there's nothing apparently wrong with the body. Some people experience excruciating pain such as constant migraines or sharp pains in their feet or legs. For others, it's a dull, nagging pain. Both types make it hard for people to live and enjoy life. It may be caused by other diseases like diabetes, HIV, fibromyalgia, or arthritis. There is much debate regarding using medical marijuana to treat pain. Doctors can't measure pain on a machine like they can measure so many other diseases. Because of this, scientists must rely on marijuana study participants to state how much their pain has decreased. Perhaps science will find new ways to measure pain in the future to reach more conclusive results. But until they do, we must look at the studies we have.

One very well-controlled study performed by researchers at the University of California showed a 30 percent decrease in pain for people who have nerve pain caused by HIV. Another study published in the *Journal of Pain* showed a similar 30 percent decrease in general chronic pain. A third notable study tested the ability of healthy

Studies have shown that marijuana is effective in reducing chronic pain.

participants to eat very hot peppers. It found that the use of marijuana significantly increased their ability to eat the hot peppers when those who did not receive marijuana had to instantly spit them out. This study may seem a little funny at face value. But think about how hard it is not to spit out a pepper that's too hot. Humans instinctually avoid pain and often have little control over their reactions to it. This study may be the most conclusive. It shows a clear and consistent reduction of pain.

AIDS- and Cancer-Related Nausea

Numerous studies have shown a reduction of nausea in both children and adults who have received medical marijuana. One well-controlled study showed nausea elimination in 71 percent of cancer patients receiving dronabinol, an anti-nausea medication containing THC. It's important to realize that there's no evidence to show that marijuana cures any disease. What it does is reduce symptoms so that patients can better cope with their illnesses.

Side Effects

It's very important to realize that just because marijuana has become more accepted and even respected worldwide doesn't mean there aren't risks for people using it both medically and recreationally. Individuals may react differently. And each person and his or her doctor must weigh whether or not the side effects are bad enough to make marijuana the wrong solution for a patient.

Some common short-term side effects include:

- Memory issues
- Terrible anxiety (normally with high-THC marijuana)
- **Paranoia**
- Seeing/smelling things that aren't there
- Slow reaction time/coordination challenges
- Rapid heart rate

Longer term effects typically occur only when someone abuses marijuana and neglects their family, studies, and obligations in life in order to use marijuana. These side effects include:

- Slightly lower **intelligence quotient** (IQ)
- Higher chance of dropping out of school
- Higher chance of losing their job
- Severe procrastination/lack of motivation
- Trouble learning complex things
- Chance of becoming dependent
- Depression/general dissatisfaction with life
- Relationship problems
- Cannabinoid hyperemesis syndrome and other syndromes

It's important to realize that someone may set out to use marijuana responsibly. They might then slowly sink into drug-dependence, abuse, and addiction. Before this happens, a person should take stock of what's important in life and make a choice for a better life. If someone is already experiencing these severe side effects and unable to quit, they should speak with an addiction counselor.

Anxiety and depression are common side effects of abusing marijuana.

Yet another key factor to consider is that a teen brain and an adult brain are not quite the same. No matter how smart you are, if you're under twenty-five-years-old, your brain is still growing and developing, according to scientists. That's why it's easier for teens to learn new languages and recover after a major brain-related accident. But it also means that the brain may develop differently if substances are introduced to it. A forty-year-long New Zealand study (which was discussed at the National Institute on Drug Abuse's website) found that people who start using marijuana in their teens had an average six-point IQ drop compared to people who didn't use it. And more interestingly, it found that people who didn't start using marijuana until they were adults saw only slight IQ drops.

"Essentially, patients who use marijuana very frequently for long periods of time—usually at least six months, probably most of them have been using for several years—develop sort of intractable abdominal pain and vomiting that sort of comes and goes over the course of days to weeks [cannabinoid hyperemesis syndrome). And it's really a quite miserable experience for them, and it's something that we're seeing more and more often in Colorado."

--Dr. Kennon Heard, a professor of emergency medicine and medical toxicology and pharmacology at the University of Colorado School of Medicine, in a 2017 interview on *Here & Now*

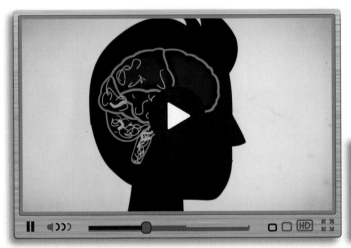

Learn more about the effects of marijuana on the teen brain:

"It doesn't have a high potential for abuse, and there are very legitimate medical applications. In fact, sometimes marijuana is the only thing that works… It is irresponsible not to provide the best care we can as a medical community, care that could involve marijuana. We have been terribly and systematically misled for nearly seventy years in the United States, and I apologize for my own role in that."

—Dr. Sanjay Gupta, neurosurgeon/CNN correspondent in a 2013 article, "Why I Changed My Mind on Weed" at CNN.com

A survey of physicians by the New England Journal of Medicine *found that nearly 80 percent of doctors worldwide support the use of medical marijuana.*

What Medical Professionals Are Saying in the U.S. and Around the World

Physicians at the *New England Journal of Medicine* surveyed doctors worldwide in seventy-two countries. They spoke with doctors in all fifty states of the United States and all ten provinces in Canada, in addition to a wide range of doctors in other countries and territories. They found that nearly eight out of ten doctors worldwide support the use of medical marijuana. Outliers exist. For example, in Utah, only 1 percent of doctors support it. In Pennsylvania, 96 percent support it. But overwhelmingly, this extensive survey shows that a shift has begun in the medical community. As more studies are completed and more patients report benefits, many doctors are recognizing the benefits. And, more importantly, for those who advocate for legalization, medical doctors are willing to speak up and announce that they support it. Why do you think that doctors are more willing to show their support now compared to ten or twenty years ago?

"Physicians in favor of medicinal marijuana often focused on our responsibility as caregivers to alleviate suffering. Many pointed out the known dangers of prescription narcotics, supported patient choice, or described personal experience with patients who benefited from the use of marijuana. Those who opposed the use of medicinal marijuana targeted the lack of evidence, the lack of provenance, inconsistency of dosage, and concern about side effects,

including psychosis. Common in this debate was the question of whether marijuana even belongs within the purview of physicians or whether the substance should be legalized and patients allowed to decide for themselves whether to make use of it."

— Jonathan N. Adler, M.D., and James A. Colbert, M.D., in "Medicinal Use of Marijuana — Polling Results," which appeared in the *New England Journal of Medicine* in 2013

"The evidence is overwhelming that marijuana can relieve certain types of pain, nausea, vomiting, and other symptoms caused by such illnesses as multiple sclerosis, cancer, and AIDS or by the harsh drugs sometimes used to treat them. And it can do so with remarkable safety. Indeed, marijuana is less toxic than many of the drugs that physicians prescribe every day."

—Joycelyn Elders, a pediatrician and the first African American appointed as Surgeon General of the United States, 2004

"The introduction of smokeless cannabis in dosage form will immediately ease human pain and suffering and help to move medical marijuana from the underground economy to the mainstream of the nation's health-care system."

—Steven R. Patierno, Ph.D., faculty member in the Duke University School of Medicine

"Cannabis impairs your ability to safely drive a vehicle. It impairs your reaction time. It impairs your ability to multitask and pay attention. Whether it's tobacco or cannabis, there are concerns with smoking anything."

—Dr. Amy Porath, the director of research and policy for the Canadian Centre on Substance Abuse, in a 2017 article about marijuana in *The Globe and Mail*

text-dependent questions

1. Which was the first state in the U.S. to legalize medical marijuana?
2. Why is the "hot pepper study" so significant?
3. Are there long-term side effects of using marijuana?

research project

Read the following article: https://www.npr.org/sections/health-shots/2014/02/25/282631913/marijuana-may-hurt-the-develop-ing-teen-brain. Then research how your brain develops as you age. How can substances impact this developmental process in regard to critical thinking, emotional intelligence, and memory? Create a poster board that explains this.

The use of recreational marijuana is legal in nearly ten U.S. states and in some other countries.

words to understand

budtender: A marijuana expert and salesperson in a marijuana dispensary (shop).

probable cause: When a police officer has a good reason to suspect that someone is committing a crime. Under U.S. law, this gives a police officer the right to investigate further by searching a person or his or her car or house.

social situations: Casual situations (birthday parties, sporting events, dinners, concerts, etc.) that involve friends and family.

tax revenue: The money that governments bring in through taxes.

chapter 4

Recreational Marijuana

In the places where recreational marijuana is legal, business is booming. Businesses across industries are seeing increased profits (the money made after expenses are paid out). People are benefiting from increased **tax revenues** now that recreational marijuana can be sold legally and taxed. But does recreational marijuana also have a "bad side?"

In this chapter, we'll look at why people use recreational marijuana and why some people think it should stay illegal. We'll explore how legal recreational marijuana is shaping society and how society is shaping it. Let's take a look.

Why Do People Use Recreational Marijuana?

Aside from the medical benefits, people use recreational marijuana to feel certain mental effects that they get when using. For some, this is a feeling of relaxation. For others, it's a feeling of giddiness. Some people feel more comfortable in **social situations** when using marijuana. Others use marijuana to help them sleep. Some people "zone out," becoming zombie-like, staring into space or not responding to those around them. For most people, a high feeling comes first, followed by the stoned, "zoned out" feeling.

Some people use marijuana in very small amounts all day, every day. These people don't get the same effects as people who consume large amounts of marijuana. Regular consumers use it so long that it just makes them feel "normal." The drug becomes the "new normal" for them. They may feel angry or irritable when they stop. If these people choose, they can quit and over a short time, they will begin to feel normal again without marijuana.

When a person uses a lot of marijuana all at once, they lose their ability to function. Some people like this out-of-control feeling. They may not be able to catch a ball that is thrown to them. They might fall over or say silly things. It's funny to them and others. It may seem fun. But it can also be very dangerous when marijuana is not used responsibly. When someone is in this state, they may have trouble making smart decisions. This may lead them to accidents, injuries, and even death. Trying to work, cook, ride a bike, or drive in this state, for example, can cause serious injury to the user or others.

Then there are people who have adverse (negative) reactions—such as paranoia, anxiety, or an inability to sleep— to marijuana. These people may not enjoy the effects of marijuana and choose to quit. They may also choose to try different kinds of marijuana that have different effects.

"I have been instructed by the board of trustees of the American Medical Association (AMA) to protest on behalf of the association against the enactment in its present form of so much of H.R. 6906 as relates to the medicinal use of cannabis and its preparations and derivatives... Since the medicinal use of cannabis has not caused and is not causing addiction, the prevention of the use of the drug for medicinal purposes can accomplish no good end whatsoever. How far it may serve to deprive the public of the benefits of a drug that on further research may prove to be of substantial value, it is impossible to foresee. The AMA has no objection to any reasonable regulation of the medicinal use of cannabis and its preparations and derivatives. It does protest, however, against being called upon to pay a special tax, to use special order forms to procure the drug, to keep special records concerning its professional use and to make special returns to the Treasury Department officials, as a condition precedent to the use of cannabis in the practice of medicine in the several States, all separate and apart from the taxes, order forms, records, and reports required under the Harrison Narcotics Act with reference to opium and coca leaves and their preparations and derivatives."

—William C. Woodward, legislative counsel of the American Medical Association in 1937 testimony to Congress in opposition to the Marijuana Tax Act

Learn more about the negative physical effects caused by using medical marijuana:

Anti-Marijuana Posters

Here are some of the headlines of anti-marijuana posters of the 1930s, a time when public opinion was changing about its use:

- "Marihuana: Assassin of Youth. A Puff. A Party. A Tragedy."
- "Marihuana: Weed with Roots in Hell"
- "Reefer Madness: Women Cry for It. Men Die for It."
- "Doped Youths: A Puff of Smoke Changed Their Lives"
- "Devil's Harvest. The Smoke of Hell! A Vicious Racket with Its Arms Around Your Children!"

Why Are Some People Against Recreational Marijuana?

Until the middle of the nineteenth century, medical marijuana use was very common in the United States. In the early twentieth century, rumors began to spread that people who used marijuana became violent and even killed people. Books and movies of the time supported this viewpoint. This scared people who didn't know that much of it was based on misinformation.

With the passage of the Marijuana Tax Act in 1937, these fears pushed people to make it illegal. At the time, the American Medical Association opposed the new law because its physician members believed that marijuana provided real medical benefits. Some people who are against marijuana today oppose it because of the misinformation that has been spread for years about the drug. Others are concerned about the real negative side effects that abusing marijuana can cause, as we discussed in the last chapter. They don't see a reason to make something legal that has these side effects. They are concerned that it will be easier for teens to have access to marijuana, although there are strict laws that prohibit its use. We discussed in the last chapter how that can have lifelong negative effects.

"Anyone 21 and older can buy and consume marijuana when you're in California, regardless of whether you're a resident of the state or just visiting. It's called 'recreational' marijuana, to distinguish it from 'medical' marijuana, which requires a doctor's recommendation. Stores must keep youngsters off the premises, and the cannabis products must be sold in child-resistant containers to reduce the risk of accidental ingestion by curious kids."

—"What California's Legalization of Marijuana Means for You," *USA Today*, 2017

Taxes collected from the sale of legal marijuana go toward road repair and other projects and programs that help the public.

Tax Revenues & Programs

Whether we're talking about a country, a state, a province, or a city, people rely on money that the government collects through taxes. Taxes help pay for the things that they share as a people. Tax revenues go toward things like funding schools, paving roads, medical care for those who can't afford it, and so on. There are taxes on the money that people make from working. There are taxes when you buy something. The taxes collected depend on the rules in that area. Businesses pay taxes and people pay taxes.

Increased tax revenues are a big deal to people and communities. When recreational marijuana is sold illegally on the black market, it can't be taxed. When it's sold in pharmacies or in dispensaries, the government can tax it. More people working also means that there are more people's incomes that can be taxed. But just how much extra tax revenue does recreational marijuana generate? Let's look at a state in the U.S. where it's been legal since 2014 as a case study.

According to its website, the state of Colorado in the United States generated just under $200 million in marijuana taxes in 2016. This was double from the year before. In 2017, it raised $247 million in taxes. For reference, alcohol brought in about $45 million in 2017, and cigarettes, $158 million. What do they do with all this money?

According to the state, around $40 million goes to the school system. Everyone benefits from better schools. About $18 million goes to public health. This includes programs that warn youth of the dangers of using marijuana and those that treat people who are misusing marijuana. Approximately $3 million dollars goes to the agricultural (farming) industry to research better ways to grow food and marijuana. And $1 million goes to the legal system to help try and convict people who break the laws. The rest goes in smaller amounts to various state projects.

In states where recreational marijuana is legal, some expenses have gone up. The rates of disability claims and workplace injury claims are higher. This costs taxpayers and employers money. This extra expense will need to be weighed in addition to evaluating related laws that could reduce this impact.

"Taxes are what we pay for civilized society."
—Oliver Wendell Holmes, Jr., U.S. Supreme Court Justice (1902–1932)

Job Growth & Unemployment

The legalization of recreational marijuana impacts more than just growers and sellers. There's a whole infrastructure needed to support the safe and efficient production and sale of marijuana.

There are many career opportunities available in the legal marijuana industry, including bud trimmer.

Let's look at how this job growth is playing out for real people across industries. In 2016, the most recent year calculated, 123,000 jobs were added to the American economy thanks to recreational marijuana. Most of these jobs were in Colorado, Washington, and other states where recreational marijuana is legal. This number includes the jobs closely related to the industry such as:

- Store owners
- **Budtender**
- Growers
- Edibles marijuana products manufacturing workers
- Marijuana restaurant chef (yes, it's a real job)

What's not so easy to calculate are the number of jobs in other industries that would not exist without legalized marijuana. These include new jobs in:

- Accounting
- Legal services
- Utilities
- Web design
- Marketing
- Writing
- Packaging and printing companies
- Childcare services

Marijuana industry professionals don't just work on farms and in dispensaries. Demand is also strong for financial workers such as accountants.

And the list goes on. In December 2017, the unemployment rate in Colorado was only 2.9 percent, according to the Colorado Department of Labor and Employment, 1.2 percent lower than the national average. On the other hand, Oregon's unemployment rate matched that of the national average, while Washington State's was actually higher than the national average. Many other factors contribute to the unemployment rate. But having fewer people out of work could be a good sign that

Putting People to Work

A report from New Frontier Data in 2017 makes an astounding prediction for 2020. It estimates that 300,000 new jobs could be created in the United States because of marijuana legalization. This increase in jobs comes at a time when manufacturing (factory) jobs are declining in the United States. This has left many lifelong factory workers out of work. For these workers, the medical and recreational marijuana industry provides an opportunity to find a good career. Experts believe that people across industries will see new opportunities for better-paying jobs as the legal marijuana industry continues to blossom.

legalizing marijuana is benefiting certain states or regions. According to the *Los Angeles Times*, Governor John Hickenlooper of Colorado once called legalizing recreational marijuana "reckless." But seeing is believing. After seeing the benefits that the state has realized, he most recently said "If I had that magic wand now, I don't know if I would wave it [to undo legalization]...It's beginning to look like it might work."

"Colorado is known for many great things... Marijuana should not be one of them."

—John Hickenlooper, governor of Colorado, in a 2012 statement

"When voters made Colorado the first state in the nation to legalize recreational marijuana in 2012, law enforcement was presented with a new challenge: understanding and enforcing new laws that aim to regulate marijuana use, rather than enforcing laws that deem marijuana use to be illegal. Supporters of the new law claimed this would make things easier for police and save at least $12 million in taxpayer dollars on reduced law enforcement costs. Agencies across the state argue that has not been the case. The legislation to enact the new laws has been vague, and consequently difficult to enforce. Unforeseen problems have arisen, ranging from how to determine when a driver is legally under the influence of marijuana to how to deal with legal drug refining operations in residential neighborhoods. Some Colorado law enforcement agencies have at least one full-time officer dedicated to marijuana regulation and enforcement, but most agencies do not have this option and are struggling to deal with the additional workload brought by legalized marijuana. Many law enforcement leaders are frustrated by the conflict between enforcing the new law and upholding federal statutes that continue to view marijuana use as illegal."

—Colorado's Legalization of Marijuana and the Impact on Public Safety: A Practical Guide for Law Enforcement, 2015

Public Safety

Does legalizing recreational marijuana help or hurt public safety? While it may reduce the crime of growing, buying, or selling marijuana illegally, does it create other public health concerns? To answer this, we'll turn to an extensive report, *Colorado's Legalization of Marijuana and the Impact on Public Safety: A Practical Guide for Law Enforcement*, from the Police Foundation, a national law enforcement organization in the United States. It did some extensive research on the impact of legalization on public safety in Colorado. In its report, the foundation identifies the following concerns:

Colorado Governor John Hickenlooper once opposed the legalization of recreational marijuana, but has changed his opinion to some degree after seeing the tax revenue that has been collected from its sale.

- The city of Denver, Colorado, in the United States, has seen an increase in the number of homeless people in the eighteen-to-twenty-six age range. The foundation doesn't believe that the legalization has caused the homelessness. Rather, it believes that Denver has become a magnet for homeless people in other states who go to Denver to access legal marijuana. An increase in the number of homeless people can put a strain on police, attempting to keep the homeless community and others safe at night.

- Yet another concern that the foundation identifies is the fact that marijuana businesses keep a lot of cash in their stores. Because marijuana is still illegal at the federal level, many banks refuse to provide services to people who buy and sell marijuana. This means that people can't use their credit or debit cards like they would in other businesses. They must pay in cash. Because of this, businesses who legally sell recreational marijuana are prime targets for armed robbers.

- Finally, the report points out the fact that marijuana is illegal at the federal level but legal at the state level. This makes it difficult to apply some laws that protect citizens. For example, U.S. citizens are protected from unlawful searches under the U.S. Constitution. A police officer must have **probable cause** to search someone's home or car when they suspect that a crime is being committed. Federal law says that the presence of marijuana gives an officer the legal right to search. But if marijuana is legal in a state, then having marijuana doesn't really suggest that a person is doing anything criminal.

In each of these concerns, the problem exists primarily because recreational marijuana is legal in some states and not in others. Denver is only a magnet because it's illegal in nearby states and at the federal level. Bank executives don't want to work with marijuana businesses because it's illegal at the federal level. They're afraid of going to prison because they would be breaking U.S. laws. It's important to recognize that all public safety concerns in the report are a direct result of the differences between state and federal laws.

"The absence and lack of data is absolutely a killer to demonstrate whether there is {sic} going to be adverse consequences of marijuana on your community or not. So what every law enforcement agency in the country should do right now, today, is start collecting data, not just on marijuana but on all controlled substances to establish a baseline. Colorado has missed their opportunity to collect baseline data, but other states could be establishing their baselines now."

—Sergeant Jim Gerhardt, Colorado Police Department

Society

In addition to those concerns noted in the report, we also have many societal benefits to consider. These are very interesting. And they will become clearer over time as more states and countries measure the before and after effects as Sergeant Gerhardt suggests in his quote.

By legalizing the most commonly used illegal substance and regulating it, the laws are taking marijuana out of the shadows. They're allowing people who choose to use to have a safer way to do so. This means less potential for crime.

States that legalize recreational marijuana can reduce the cost of many services. These are only necessary because marijuana is illegal in some places. They include the cost of arresting, detaining, trying, and imprisoning people who use and sell marijuana. This not only results in saving money. It also includes the impact that imprisonment has on families and people. In prison, people often learn how to become better criminals, which is bad for society. By reducing the number of people we're sending to prison for "low-level" drug offenses we're cutting off the flow of criminals. This book is in no way suggesting that we shouldn't imprison people who break laws. But, more and more, society is realizing that putting nonviolent offenders away for years isn't the answer. It destroys families and communities. But we're changing strategies to include treating addiction while permitting safe use of marijuana. Over time, states should see the results of a lower prison population throughout communities.

Environment

It's a topic that people who oppose or support marijuana rarely bring up. But legalizing recreational marijuana is often bad for the environment. Marijuana grows wild in places like India as we've discussed in earlier chapters. But, in most places, marijuana must be deliberately grown outdoors or in indoor grow facilities.

Let's look at how producing marijuana on a large scale impacts the environment.

A marijuana plant uses about six gallons (twenty-three liters) per day, which is double what most other similar crops need. This will require significant shifting of water supplies. It may take water away from other places like streams and rivers where fish and other animals need that water to survive. Many forests that help clean the air and provide animals with places to live may be cut down to make room for marijuana fields. This could cause an increase in carbon dioxide, which many believe contributes to global warming.

A 2012 government report found that around 3 percent of California energy was being used to grow marijuana. In countries such as Canada, where the average day is much cooler than the U.S., the energy usage to keep outdoor plants from freezing is even higher.

The environmental effects of large-scale marijuana farming must be carefully considered before more U.S. states and other countries legalize marijuana.

Environmental Pros and Cons of Growing Marijuana

"Weed plants are thirsty. A 2016 working document prepared for the Oregon State Legislature reported that a single mature weed plant can consume almost six gallons (twenty-three liters) of water per day, compared to about three-and-a-half gallons (thirteen liters) for a wine grape plant. That fact matters especially in dry regions and seasons, which we'll likely see extended in the coming decades from climate change."

—James Wilt, "Growing Weed Is Pretty Bad for the Environment, " Vice.com, 2017

"Smoking marijuana has some environmental downsides. But there are many other far more serious personal behaviors from an environment and climate point of view, such as driving large internal-combustion vehicles like trucks and SUVs, or air travel, or consuming large quantities of factory-farmed meat."

—James Wilt, "Growing Weed Is Pretty Bad for the Environment,"Vice.com, 2017

text-dependent questions

1. At what age does your brain stop developing?
2. Is marijuana legal everywhere for medical use?
3. At what age is marijuana legal in most U.S. states?

research project

Use the internet to learn more about how marijuana is being used to treat epilepsy. Watch videos, gather information from the Epilepsy Foundation, and write a short report on different treatments, including marijuana, and their effectiveness.

In 2016, 57 percent of adults in the U.S. who were surveyed by The Pew Research Center believed that marijuana should be legal.

words to understand

addiction: A state of being unable to stop something that is negatively impacting one's life.

cultivation: The growing of a plant.

data collection: Gathering information about something so that you can compare it to information collected later. By doing this we can reach conclusions about how something, such as marijuana legalization, impacted a place or people.

unicorn: In the business world, a start-up (new company) that is valued at more than $1 billion. It's important to remember that while many unicorns grow to become successful and highly-valued companies, others do not grow and lose their value.

chapter 5

The Future of Marijuana

Alcohol was once completely prohibited (banned) in the United States. And it still is in some counties and towns. Today, use among responsible adults is socially accepted in most settings and places. For most people, alcohol is not a big deal. It only becomes an issue when people act recklessly while intoxicated (drunk). When they put themselves and others at risk, there are consequences. Alcohol only becomes illegal when people break the laws that apply to it such as underage drinking or driving while intoxicated. These laws help keep people safe. They punish this reckless behavior. But otherwise, people are free to do what they want. Will we see and treat marijuana the same way in five to ten years? In this chapter, we'll explore the future of marijuana.

Additional Research and Evidence of Health Benefits

As barriers begin to fall, many believe further research will be conducted and supported by the federal government. In the very short term, industry experts predict that there may be resistance within the federal government of the United States. This resistance may continue to make it harder to research marijuana. Remember that statement we saw earlier from Attorney General Jeff Sessions? But the ball is already rolling. Important U.S. agencies like the Food & Drug Administration (FDA) are stating their support for research going forward.

In the short run, we'll still see those fighting back against legalization such as the Drug Enforcement Agency (DEA) in the United States. Until federal law changes, this will continue to be the official position of these organizations.

"The agency works closely with the medical and patient communities, and our federal partners when necessary, to allow access to experimental treatments...The Food & Drug Administration (FDA) also has an important role to play in supporting scientific research into the medical uses of marijuana and its constituents in scientifically valid investigations as part of the agency's drug review and approval process. As a part of this role, the FDA supports those in the medical research community who intend to study marijuana."

—United States FDA website

*"Marijuana is the only major drug of abuse grown within the U.S. borders. The Drug Enforcement Administration is aggressively striving to halt the spread of cannabis **cultivation** in the United States."*

—Drug Enforcement Administration website

Greater Access for Patients

The easing of restrictions and the FDA's support of research will give greater access to marijuana for medical usage. Many people could benefit from marijuana. But they are hesitant to use it because it's illegal where they live. Once marijuana becomes legal, they will be able to make the choice for themselves. Medical marijuana will become yet another potential treatment option for those patients.

Marijuana advocates hope that new research being conducted on the benefits of marijuana will help the drug to become better integrated into medical treatment plans.

"Possession arrests and convictions can have devastating effects on users and their families—especially for young men of color, who are disproportionately targeted, and for immigrants, who can be deported for a criminal offense. There are a number of additional sanctions associated with drug convictions; for example, they can make it harder to receive federal aid for college, or access public housing. The stigma around criminalization can also make it harder for users to get help or discuss their problems with family members and health professionals."

—Beau Kilmer, codirector of the RAND Drug Policy Research Center, and Robert MacCoun, The James and Patricia Kowal Professor of Law at Stanford University

More Focus on Education About Responsible Use and Addiction Treatment

Places that legalize marijuana for either medical or recreational use will set aside a portion of the tax revenue that is generated. (Taxes are fees imposed by the government on people and businesses; they help pay for government services.) These funds will support more effective drug treatment programs. People who abuse marijuana and other drugs will have greater access to treatment for **addiction**. We'll put more emphasis on educating people about making smart

A portion of the tax revenue collected for the sale of legal marijuana is being used to pay for programs that help people who become addicted to the drug.

decisions. We'll put more trust in people to make their own choices. For some, the choice will be not to use marijuana. For others, the choice will be to use it responsibly. And yet others will break the laws that society establishes. They will face the penalties. Right now, many countries are spending time and money trying to arrest people who are using marijuana in a responsible way. Soon, we'll refocus our efforts on helping people who don't use it responsibly and become addicted.

"This is an excellent time to remind parents, students, educators, administrators, and the public about the detrimental effects of marijuana, especially to the developing brains of children. In this new environment we need to be even more vigilant in making certain school-aged children understand the importance of making healthy decisions. We are committed to making sure that new resources will effectively support schools, families, and communities in this charge."

—Tom Torlakson, state superintendent of public instruction in California, in response to the passage of Proposition 64, which legalized the recreational use of cannabis for adults 21 and older

"Decisions about price and profit motive will ultimately shape how legalization affects public health and public safety..."

—Beau Kilmer, codirector of the RAND Drug Policy Research Center, a non-partisan research center

"If we think them not enlightened enough to exercise their control with wholesome discretion, the remedy is not to take it from them but to inform their discretion by education."

—Thomas Jefferson, U.S. President, 1801–1809

Better Data Collection to Compare Before and After

Many believe that before and after **data collection** has been lacking. Because of this, they think that we may not be seeing the negative effects that legalization is causing. We have little to measure. This lack of "before" data is at least partially due to the fact that places that have legalized marijuana didn't know what they should be measuring. And secondly, it's due to the fact that the change in public perception that led to actual policy changes came so quickly. In haste to legalize, many have lost the opportunities to gather data. Without it, it's hard to properly measure and

Some people believe that legal marijuana may replace alcohol as America's "drug of choice."

address any "negatives" that have arisen from legalization. We can expect that those regions that have been slower to "get on the bandwagon" can gather more meaningful data. This data will help protect the public and shape policies.

"It is too early to draw any conclusions about the potential effects of marijuana legalization or commercialization on public safety, public health, or youth outcomes and this may always be difficult due to the lack of historical data."

—Jack Reed, statistical analyst, Colorado Division of Criminal Justice, 2016

Could Marijuana Replace Alcohol as the "Drug of Choice?"

People will soon have greater access to legal marijuana around the world. As this happens, people who are using other drugs may increasingly turn to marijuana as their drug of choice. A drug of choice is just a term that means "preferred substance." A person's drug of choice could be social media, video games, exercise, caffeine, etc. For many adults the drug of choice is alcohol, if used responsibly. Some believe that marijuana is a better option than alcohol for relaxation and other mental benefits. While alcohol causes hangovers and sometimes aggression, marijuana has a more mellowing effect on most people.

Fifty-one percent of millennials (those born between 1982 and 2004), prefer marijuana to alcohol, according to a report from Monocle Research and OutCo, a Southern California-based cannabis company. If this trend continues, could marijuana replace alcohol usage around the world? In addition, as we've previously discussed, people who use dangerous opioids prefer marijuana to treat pain.

See how Arizona dispensaries are combatting marijuana side effects by better labeling packaging:

Many marijuana products are now available.

More Marijuana Products

We've seen it in places where recreational marijuana is already legal. There is tremendous opportunity for inventors to find new and interesting ways to put marijuana in their products. We will see marijuana-infused fruit juice, lotions, and tinctures. We'll likely see new technologies developed around marijuana. Laws similar to those for alcohol and tobacco will be put into place to prevent advertising directly to children or teens. These laws will also need to put barriers in place to prevent underage individuals from buying certain products. But other products will be deemed safe and have no age limits. Products that contain cannabidiol (CBD) may eventually be available without an age limit. CBD is a chemical found in marijuana that doesn't have the severe mental effects.

Speaking about industry opportunities in marijuana in 2017, Sullivan told investors "There are many **unicorns** *to come, and unicorns are those billion-dollar companies."*

—Jeanne Sullivan, venture capital investor and co-founder of StarVest Partners

"Sooner or later, you're going to be able to say, 'Alexa, send me an eighth of flower."

—George Blankenship, former Tesla and Apple executive, 2017

Will More Countries Legalize Marijuana for Both Medical and Recreational Use?

Many countries are watching and waiting. They are ready to legalize marijuana. But they hope to see how it works for others first. They don't want to have to recreate the wheel. In their more measured response, they'd prefer to allow others to make mistakes. They know that by making mistakes countries will learn the best way to regulate and tax the industry. Their own countries can then apply this knowledge to develop their own policies. The results coming out of places where it has been legalized are promising enough for others to take notice.

"…the states' economies are feeling the effects [of the marijuana industry] on real estate, the effects on the job market, the effects on travel and hospitality, and the effects from a reduction in taxpayer burden from the criminal justice system."

—Leslie Bocskor, Electrum Partners, 2017

Prominent Politicians Who've Shown Support for Legalization in the U.S.

"That is not a drug. It's a leaf."

—Arnold Schwarzenegger, actor/former governor of California, 2007

"I think that most small amounts of marijuana have been decriminalized in some places, and should be. We really need a re-examination of our entire policy on imprisonment…Our imprisonment policies are counter-productive."

—Bill Clinton, U.S. president, 2000

"Look, I've been very clear about my belief that we should try to discourage substance abuse. And I am not somebody who believes that legalization is a panacea. But I do believe that treating this as a public-health issue, the same way we do with cigarettes or alcohol, is the much smarter way to deal with it."

—Barack Obama, U.S. president, 2017

"If somebody's gonna smoke a joint in their house and not do anybody else any harm, then perhaps there are other things that our cops should be looking at to engage in and try to clean up some of the other problems that we have in society.""

—Sarah Palin, former governor of Alaska, 2010

Easing Up on Travel Restrictions

It's currently difficult to fly or cross borders with marijuana even if someone has a medical card authorizing it. People who need medical marijuana to treat the symptoms of conditions such as epilepsy cannot travel. But if marijuana becomes legal in the U.S. at the federal level and more countries legalize it, people will be able to travel with this drug. Some countries may be slower to allow travel with recreational marijuana. But medical marijuana is quickly becoming tolerated.

In 2012, then-President Obama said, "The War on Drugs has been an utter failure. We need to rethink and decriminalize our marijuana laws."

Next Locations to Legalize Marijuana in Some Form

Canada planned to permit the growing, selling, and purchasing of medical and recreational marijuana in 2018. The legal age to buy will vary by province. It's typically around age nineteen.

Mexico legalized medical marijuana in June 2017. It is preparing to make it legal for recreational use in early 2018 on a limited basis. It will be permitted in food, drink, and other specified products. Mexico doesn't plan to legalize the growing, buying, or selling of recreational marijuana in its natural state. Rather, it plans to import products being manufactured elsewhere. There are indications that full legalization with regulation and taxes may follow. Mexico is grappling with a terrible drug-trafficking problem. Drug trafficking is the selling of illegal drugs; violence often occurs

Mexican President Enrique Peña Nieto (above left) previously opposed legalizing cannabis, but began to change his opinion of legalization after seeing the success of legalization efforts in the United States and in other countries. "I'm not ruling out that in the near future marijuana will be fully legalized in Mexico. It's already occurring in other countries, particularly the United States," he said in a 2017 interview in Cultura Colectiva."

as drug cartels, or gangs, battle for territory. Much of this is marijuana-related. The United States is the drug cartel's biggest customer. The sale of marijuana and other drugs generates huge profits for drug cartels. If the U.S. legalizes marijuana at the federal level, it will help undercut the drug trade in Mexico, cutting off its money and power. Mexico also hopes to undercut the drug trade with this move toward legalization.

[Legalization] "is the very first step to start taking away from cartels all the money they get from this illegal activity. This is a slow process, but I'm sure it will happen one day soon."
—Vicente Fox, former President of Mexico, *Rolling Stone*, 2017

Colombia in South America will likely be among the next countries to legalize marijuana. It has dealt with dangerous drug cartels for decades. And like its neighbors, Mexico and Uruguay, it hopes that legalization will reduce the power of these violent gangs.

Jamaica, an island country in the Caribbean, currently has legalized medical marijuana. It appears that very soon it will legalize recreational marijuana as well. This country has suffered from terrible poverty. Government officials hope that legalization will bring new tourism into the area. Tourists buy everything from food and lodging, to souvenirs and tickets to lavish tours. Government officials hope that they will eventually purchase both recreational and medical marijuana, too. Tourists can bring millions of dollars and other currencies into Jamaica. This will create new jobs and help raise the standard of living.

Italy is in the process of moving toward legalization of recreational marijuana. Marijuana legalization supporters have collected 68,000 signatures demanding that their government review marijuana policy. It's still early. But given how fast other countries have moved, we may see legalization within a few years.

In the Czech Republic, marijuana has been decriminalized. This means that many of the harsher penalties have been removed. Medical marijuana is also legal. Legalizing medical marijuana and decriminalizing recreational are steps. They move the country toward full legalization of recreational marijuana. Like Jamaica, officials in this European country hope to become a tourist destination for those who enjoy using marijuana recreationally.

France is beginning its move toward legalization. Like the U.S., many people are questioning why the country has such long prison sentences for marijuana usage and sales. Some of those in leadership are now working toward meeting the will of the people. They are supporting decriminalization of marijuana on the road to full legalization.

The Hype Dies Down

Some people are very excited about the possibility of legalization. Others are already in places where marijuana is legal. As the "newness" of legal cannabis wears off, we can expect there to be less talk about it. Dispensaries will become commonplace. Some people will choose to use it. Others will decide that they'd rather live a cleaner lifestyle that doesn't include substances that alter the mind. There will be some who use it responsibly and others who need treatment for addiction and abuse.

Even after it's fully legal in more areas, some people will still oppose it, much like some people are against cigarettes or alcohol. Government officials will continue to evaluate the pros and cons and put policies in place that allow more personal freedom while protecting the public at the same time.

text-dependent questions

1. What is the Food and Drug Administration's official position on researching medical marijuana?
2. How might legalization of recreational marijuana throughout the U.S. impact Mexico's drug cartel problems?
3. How might legalization impact travel from state to state and country to country?

research project

How do you see marijuana's future in the next five years where you live? Will it be legal? How will it impact society and education? What new laws might we need to keep people safe? How might it change the face of advertising? What should communities do to prevent access and abuse by minors? Consider these and other issues that may arise. On a poster board, add pictures and other items that represent the future of marijuana where you live. Be ready to discuss your work.

series glossary of key terms

adult-use cannabis: The recreational use of cannabis by those over the age of twenty-one.

cannabidiol (CBD): A chemical compound found in the cannabis plant that is non-psychoactive. It is known for its medical and pain relief properties.

cannabinoid: Any of various chemical compounds (such as THC) from the cannabis or marijuana plant that produces a euphoric feeling, or "high."

cannabis clubs: Marijuana growing and consumption cooperatives (a group that is owned and run by its members) that exist in countries such as Uruguay and Spain to provide cannabis users with marijuana products and a place to use those products.

cannabis strains: Varieties of cannabis plants that are developed to have different properties and potencies.

clinical trials: Experiments with unproven medications that may or may not help a patient get better.

dabbing: A somewhat controversial method of cannabis flash-vaporization. It has very strong effects on the user.

decriminalization: The legal term for getting rid of or reducing criminal charges for having or using cannabis.

delta-9-tetrahydrocannabinol (THC): A natural chemical compound found in the flowers of the marijuana plant. It produces a feeling of euphoria and a psychoactive reaction, or "high," when marijuana is eaten or smoked.

dopamine: A naturally occurring chemical in the human body that increases pleasurable feelings in the mind and body.

drug trafficking: A global illegal trade involving the growth, manufacture, distribution, and sale of substances, such as cannabis, that are subject to drug prohibition laws.

edible: A food made or infused (cooked or otherwise prepared) with cannabis extracts (portions of the plant, including seeds or flowers).

endocannabinoid system: A group of cannabinoid receptors found in the brain and central and peripheral nervous systems of mammals that help control appetite, pain, mood, and memory.

euphoria: A feeling of intense well-being and happiness.

extracts: Portions of the marijuana plant, including seeds or flowers.

hash: A solid or resinous extract of cannabis.

hemp: A cannabis plant grown for its fiber and used to make rope, textiles, paper, and other products.

ingest: To take food, drink, or another substance into the body.

lethargy: Lack of enthusiasm and energy; a common side effect of cannabis use.

Marihuana Tax Act of 1937: A marijuana taxation act that led to the prohibition of cannabis in the United States during much of the twentieth century.

marijuana: A cannabis plant that is smoked or consumed as a psychoactive (mind-altering) drug.

marijuana dispensary: A place where people can buy recreational or medical cannabis. Dispensaries are tightly controlled by the government.

marijuana oil: Liquid that is extracted from the hemp plant and placed in either capsule form or combined with foods or drinks. CBD is most commonly consumed as an oil.

medical cannabis identification card: A document issued by a state where it is legal to use medical cannabis; the card indicates that a patient may use, buy, or have medical cannabis at home, on his or her person, or both.

neuroprotectant: A substance that repairs and protects the nervous system, its cells, structure, and function.

neurotransmitter: Chemicals that communicate information in the human body.

opiates: Substances derived from the opium poppy plant such as heroin.

opium: A highly addictive narcotic drug that is created by collecting and drying the milky juice that comes from the seed pods of the poppy plant.

prohibition: The action of forbidding something, especially by law.

propaganda: False information that is created to influence people.

prosecution: The conducting of legal proceedings against someone if it is believed that they broke the law.

psychoactive drug: A drug that affects the mind.

psychosis: Detachment from reality.

receptors: Groups of specialized cells that can convert energy into electrical impulses.

repeal: To get rid of a law or congressional act.

shatter: Cannabis concentrate that looks like colored glass.

social cannabis use: The use of cannabis in social settings, whether in public or private.

tar: A toxic byproduct of cigarette or marijuana smoking.

tincture: A medicine made by dissolving a drug in alcohol, vinegar, or glycerites.

topicals: Cannabis-infused lotions, balms, and salves that relieve pain and aches at the application site on the body.

vaporizer: A device that is used to turn water or medicated liquid into a vapor for inhalation.

War on Drugs: An anti-drug campaign started in the United States in 1971 by then-president Richard Nixon. Its goal was to fight drug abuse and shipments of illegal drugs to the U.S. from Latin America, Mexico, and other places.

Index

Photo Credits

Further Reading & Internet Resources

Blesching, Uwe. *The Cannabis Health Index: Combining the Science of Medical Marijuana with Mindfulness Techniques to Heal 100 Chronic Symptoms and Diseases*. Berkeley, Calif.: North Atlantic Books, 2015.

DeAngelo, Steve. *The Cannabis Manifesto: A New Paradigm for Wellness*. Berkeley, Calif.: North Atlantic Books, 2015.

Hageseth, Christian, and Joseph D'Agnese. *Big Weed: An Entrepreneur's High-Stakes Adventures in the Budding Legal Marijuana Business*. New York: St. Martin's Press, 2015.

Hudak, John. *Marijuana: A Short History*. Washington, D.C.: Brookings Institution Press, 2016.

Lee, Martin A. *Smoke Signals: A Social History of Marijuana: Medical, Recreational and Scientific*. New York: Scribner, 2013.

Internet Resources

https://www.medicalmarijuanainc.com. Visit this site to stay up-to-date on the latest medical marijuana research. Read informative articles and learn what's happening at home and around the world.

https://www.drugabuse.gov/drugs-abuse/marijuana. This is the official U.S. government website for marijuana created by the National Institute on Drug Abuse. It includes a description of marijuana and its health effects, as well as statistics and information on trends and research.

http://health.canada.ca/en/services/health/campaigns/marijuana-cannabis. html. Follow Canada's move toward legalization at Canada's official government website. Officials will post the latest laws and information related to the industry here.

https://www.ganjapreneur.com/topic/entrepreneurs. Want to learn more about the legal marijuana industry? Visit this site to learn about business men and women who are investing in the marijuana business.

https://hightimes.com. This magazine may have a funny name, but it's very serious about providing up-to-date and accurate information on the quickly-changing marijuana scene. From legalization, to medical research, to the latest products, *High Times* covers it all.

About the Author:

Leigh Clayborne is a health and wellness writer who lives in Nashville, Tennessee. She graduated from the University of Mississippi with a degree in education. She has worked in the medical industry for more than ten years and has written thousands of books and articles for others during her career. She speaks Spanish and volunteers as a foreign language English teacher. She is a micro-influencer on social media and maintains a regular blog that helps medical professionals better connect with patients through the internet.

Video Credits

Chapter 1: Learn about the history of marijuana in Amsterdam: http://x-qr.net/1G1s

Chapter 2: Find out about Mayor Rahm Emanuel's stance on decriminalization in this news story: http://x-qr.net/1FoJ

Learn more about a twelve-year-old girl who uses marijuana to control her seizures who is suing Jeff Sessions and the Drug Enforcement Agency to legalize the use of medical marijuana across the country: http://x-qr.net/1DHH

Chapter 3: Learn more about the effects of marijuana on the teen brain: http://x-qr.net/1Cu4

Chapter 4: Learn more about the negative physical effects caused by using medical marijuana: http://x-qr.net/1CrM

Chapter 5: See how Arizona dispensaries are combatting marijuana side effects by better labeling packaging: http://x-qr.net/1Gmc